The Tree Farmer

Written by **Chuck Leavell**
and
Nicholas Cravotta

Illustrated by *Rebecca Bleau*

VSP Books
7402-G Lockport Place
Lorton, VA 22079

Order books through your local bookstore
or from your favorite book website
or by calling **1-800-441-1949**
or at **www.VSPBooks.com**.

ISBN 1-893622-16-9

Library of Congress Catalog Card Number: 2005935407

10 9 8 7 6 5 4 3 2 1

Printed in the United States of America

Chuck and Rose Lane Leavell
wish to dedicate this book to all of
the families that have a history of
stewardship of our forests.

The Generations of Family
Stewards of Charlane Plantation
Julia and Alton White, Sr.
Rosaline and Alton White, Jr.
Chuck and Rose Lane Leavell
our daughters, Amy and Ashley
their children and generations beyond

To Love, Our Children and The Family
-Nicholas and Rebecca

Tree
Farm

"Grandfather!" says the boy.
"I thought you lived on a farm.

You don't have very many
chickens. And where are the
cows and pigs?"

Grandfather says slowly,
"We grow trees."

"Wow! Apples or oranges?
I hope they're not figs.
Can I help you pick them?"

Grandfather smiles.
"Come. Take my hand."

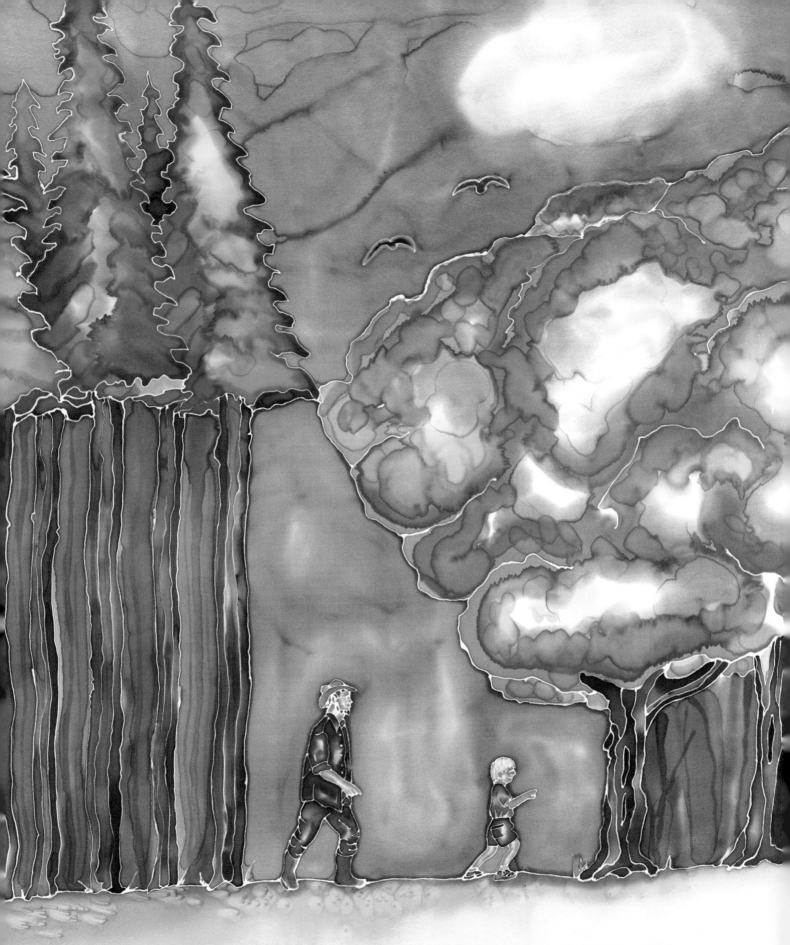

"Let me introduce you to the Pines. Look how gracefully they race
each other towards the sky. These over here are the Oaks."

"I like to think of them as the old men of the farm. And here are the Maples, whose leaves shower the earth with the most splendid colors."

"They are so beautiful," says the boy.

"Trees offer more than beauty,"
says Grandfather, watching the boy.

"These trees clean the air we breathe
and the water we drink.

Without the forests of the world, we
would not be able to live."

"Look! There's a deer passing on its way to a hidden lake," Grandfather says.

"There are many animals here who call the forest their home."

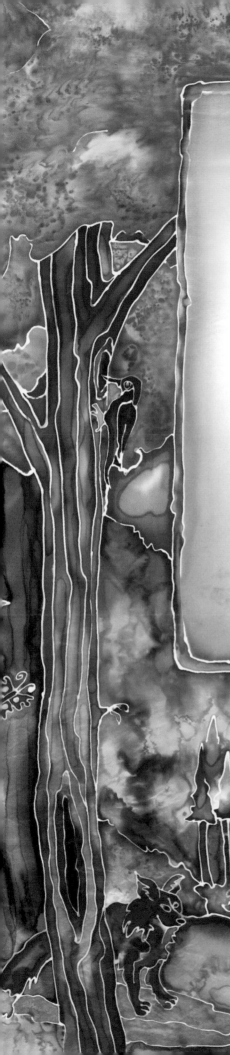

"I must tell you, there is much for me to do as I take care of the trees.

I plant them as young seedlings.

To make sure they grow strong, I trim their branches and protect them from insects and wild fire.

I am also responsible for helping keep nature in balance so that all the other plants and animals in the forest are safe and healthy."

"There is much to consider.

That is why I am so careful
as to when and how I cut
a tree down."

"You cut them down?" asks the boy.

"But why? How could you?"

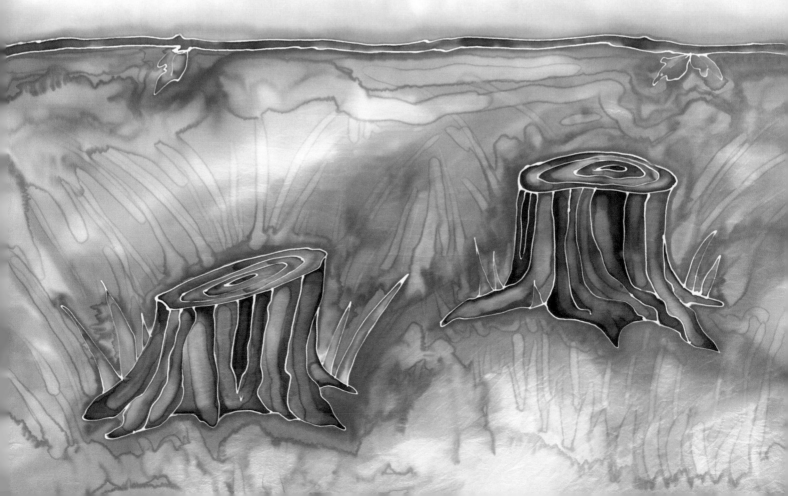

Grandfather reaches out for the nearest tree.

"This tree," he says as he runs his old
fingers over its rough bark.
"I planted it 37 years ago.
It touches my soul to stand in its shadow.
After today, it will touch souls
in a completely different way."

"Part of this tree will be made into a crib to protect a baby
and gently carry her as she dreams."

"This tree," continues Grandfather, moving to another, "will become a home for a family. It will safely house them and their memories, in joy and sadness, and shelter them at night through storms."

"This tree will become many things:

a baseball bat,
a school book,
a wooden puzzle,
a chair,
a paper airplane,
a chest of drawers,
wrapping paper,
a photograph,
wallpaper,
an artist's sketchbook,
a painting easel,
newspaper,
paper bags,
fuel for a campfire,

and even," he pauses,
"the handle of an ax
that will be used to harvest other trees."

"The life of this tree will pass to the piano to be made from its wood."

"It will join its many cousins, the violin and cello, the guitar and clarinet, the marimba and drum. It will live on in the sweetness of music, reflecting the rhythm, harmony and melody of life."

"This tree will become paper upon which many people will share their ideas, thoughts, and dreams. It will be a source of inspiration and knowledge."

Grandfather smiles sweetly. "Can you see them? Newspapers, photos, books. Even a love letter and its envelope, written with passion and sealed with endless hope to be forever treasured by she who receives it."

Grandfather closes his
eyes as he rests his
hand on the next tree.

"This tree, too,"
he says softly, "is sacred.
It is destined to become
a four-poster bed,
the place where
dreams are conceived."

"It will quiet the body
after the day's work is done
and make the spirit young
again with the promise
of a new day."

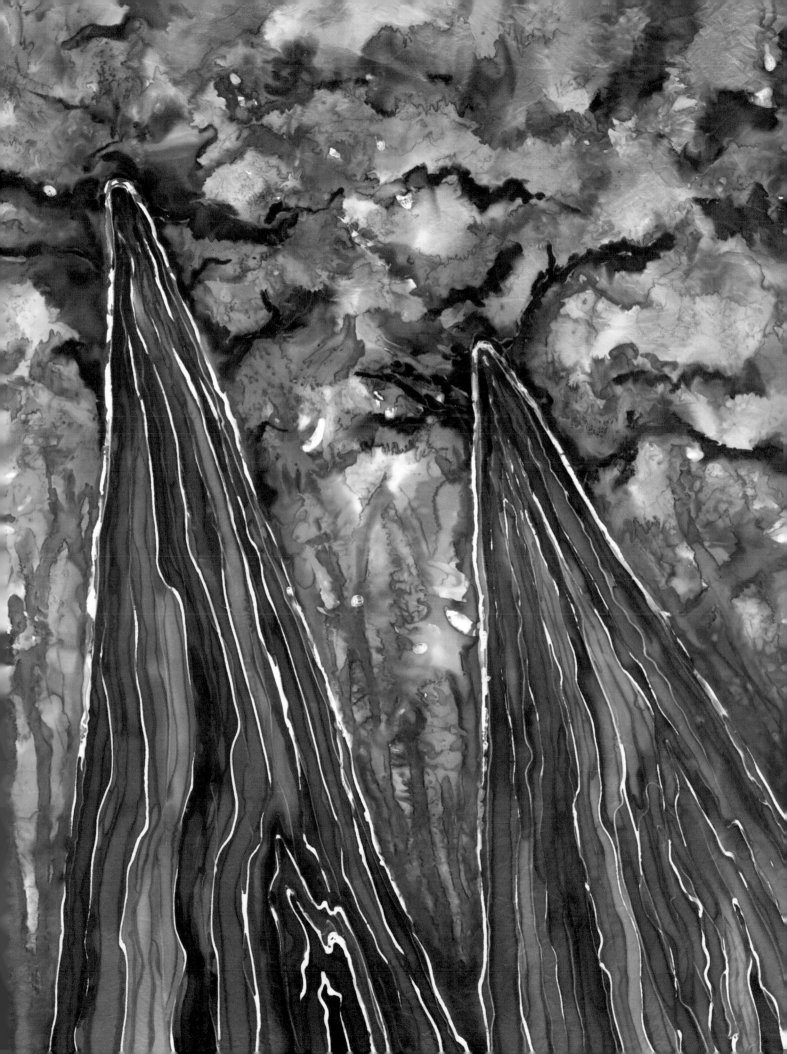

"What about this one?" asks the boy, turning to the large oak in front of the farmhouse. "What will happen to this tree?"

"This oak was here before my grandfather and will be here long after you share it with your own grandchildren."

"And I, too," Grandfather says proudly, with his hand on his own chest, "have given of myself. I am a steward of this land and have worked hard with respect and love to care for the trees."

"The land has given us her gifts for generations.

If we are reckless, we could destroy this forest,
as well as all of the animals in it.

We must remember to give of ourselves
as the forest has given to us.

If we do and we harvest the land responsibly,
there will be no end to her gifts."

Putting his hand on the head of the boy, Grandfather says softly,
"In what marvelous ways shall you give of your life, young one?"

The Tree Farmer is based on Charlane Plantation, a historic 2,200-acre tree farm in Georgia cared for by Chuck and Rose Lane Leavell. It has been passed down by family stewards from one generation to another. The book's illustrations are large silk paintings based on photographs of Charlane.

Forests make our world better in many ways. They supply us with the wood that makes our homes and furniture and the everyday paper products, such as paper towels, bags, packaging and writing paper, that have become necessities in our lives. Forests also serve as shelter from storms and homes for wildlife. Trees in a forest act as sponges, absorbing dangerous gases and other harmful pollutants. They are nature's air conditioners as well. As leaves on the trees slowly release clean water, the water draws heat from the air and cools it, keeping many of our cities and towns cooler.

To keep the forests healthy, tree farmers must protect trees from many natural dangers, including insects, disease, fires and storms. They prune branches to keep trees strong and healthy. Tree farmers also help to keep animals, birds and other creatures healthy by creating and maintaining the habitats they require. The operation of a successful and well-maintained plantation requires the dedication and hard work of an outstanding team, and Charlane Plantation is no exception. This book is dedicated in part to all of the people, both at Charlane Plantation and throughout the rest of the world, who help care for the forests and natural resources.

Visit **www.thetreefarmer.org** to learn more about this book and other ideas on how you and your family can be environmental stewards, respecting and helping to care for our environment.

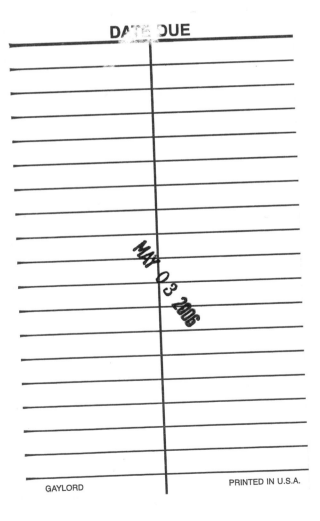

DATE DUE

MAY 03 2006

GAYLORD   PRINTED IN U.S.A.